# baby signing

*how to talk with your baby
in american sign language*

D1303051

## andrea fixell and ted stafford

### photographs by bill milne

VIKING STUDIO

VIKING STUDIO
Published by the Penguin Group
Penguin Group (USA) Inc., 375 Hudson Street,
    New York, New York 10014, U.S.A.
Penguin Group (Canada), 90 Eglinton Avenue East,
    Suite 700, Toronto, Ontario, Canada M4P 2Y3
    (a division of Pearson Penguin Canada Inc.)
Penguin Books Ltd, 80 Strand, London WC2R 0RL,
    England
Penguin Ireland, 25 St. Stephen's Green, Dublin 2,
    Ireland
    (a division of Penguin Books Ltd)
Penguin Books Australia Ltd, 250 Camberwell Road,
    Camberwell, Victoria 3124, Australia
    (a division of Pearson Australia Group Pty Ltd)
Penguin Books India Pvt Ltd, 11 Community Centre,
    Panchsheel Park, New Delhi – 110 017, India
Penguin Group (NZ), Cnr Airborne and Rosedale
    Roads, Albany, Auckland 1310, New Zealand
    (a division of Pearson New Zealand Ltd)
Penguin Books (South Africa) (Pty) Ltd,
    24 Sturdee Avenue, Rosebank, Johannesburg 2196,
    South Africa

Penguin Books Ltd, Registered Offices:
80 Strand, London WC2R 0RL, England

First published in 2006 by Viking Studio,
a member of Penguin Group (USA) Inc.

10  9  8  7  6  5  4  3  2  1

This book is intended as a fun introduction to American
Sign Language for babies and toddlers. Although the
information in this book has been developed from
American Sign Language, certain signs have been changed
to make them more accessible to your young signers.

# contents

# introduction: little fingers can say big things

**It was very early one morning**—5:30, to be exact—that the magic finally happened. Exhausted from another night of minimal sleep, Andrea was ready for her usual wake-up call. Eight-month-old Sam would soon be ready for breakfast. But this time it was different. Along with his cry, a little hand sprouted from beneath the covers, squeezing a fist over and over again—the sign for *milk*. Elated, Andrea called to her husband, stirring him from some desperately needed sleep. "He's signing! Sam's actually signing!"

Later that morning, on the other side of town, nine-month-old Zeb was enjoying a ride on Ted's chest in the front-pack carrier. Zeb was keeping an eye peeled for dogs and patting his thigh happily whenever he spotted one. Because he had learned the signs for the things he liked, Zeb was able to "talk" about his surroundings for six months before the words came.

**Parents and scientists alike** have discovered the wonders of baby signing. Researchers have found that signing babies have a stronger command of language and are more motivated to learn to speak than babies who do not sign. Parents are thrilled when their little ones can communicate their feelings and emotions before they can form words.

We have been teaching Sign-a-Song classes in Brooklyn, New York, since 2001. Our reason for teaching Sign-a-Song is quite simple: we love signing with babies and sharing the joy of their newfound language skills. Sign-a-Song incorporates a variety of songs, stories, and games to introduce signs that are relevant to a baby's life. In this book we will share some of our favorites.

All caregivers know that babies possess a preverbal vocabulary: they understand many of the words they hear, but they just can't spit them out. At the same time, babies can also recognize and remember signs. This typically happens around the sixth month. The cool thing about baby signing is that Junior has the manual dexterity to sign at eight months, whereas the skills necessary for beginning speech aren't typically developed until the twelfth month. When you begin building a connection between a gesture and a concept your baby already understands, great things can happen. Baby signing isn't really about teaching babies to communicate—they already know how to do that. It's about communicating in a language that you both can share at an earlier stage of your baby's life.

## baby signing faq

**q.** When should I start signing with my child?

**a.** It's never too early to start signing. Expect your child to sign back as early as eight months; by twelve or fourteen months, he may be signing regularly.

**q.** Will signing interfere with my child's speech development?

**a.** No. On the contrary, signing has been shown to aid speech development.

**q.** Which hand should I use to sign?

**a.** It doesn't really matter. Sign with your dominant hand unless it's otherwise occupied.

**q.** Some signs are two handed. What if I'm holding something?

**a.** Just sign with your free hand. The context should make your meaning clear.

**q.** Should I sign myself or move my child's hands?

**a.** Try them both, but make sure to show your child the sign plenty of times.

**q.** My child's sign doesn't look exactly right. Is that okay?

**a.** Yes. If you both know what it means, great.

**q.** What is the sign for Cheerios?

**a.** Make an O-hand.

**q.** How am I supposed to remember all this stuff?

**a.** The more you sign, the more you'll remember. Try incorporating your signs into songs and stories.

## spellbinding letters

The ASL alphabet is fun to learn and incredibly handy: Many signs use the first letter of the word as part of the sign.

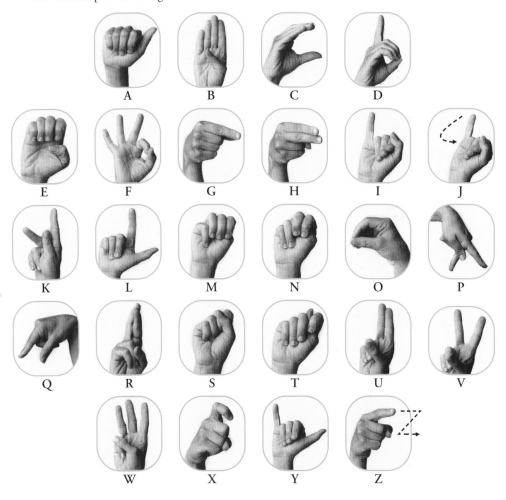

## count on it!

Like the ABCs, numbers are fun to sign and they are easy to work into games and stories.

| 1 | 2 | 3 | 4 | 5 |

| 6 | 7 | 8 | 9 | 10 |

watch out!
The sign for "three" is made with
the thumb, index, and middle fingers.
If you sign "three" with the three middle fingers
you will be making a "W" instead.

▲ look it up!
**double digits** Need the sign for *11, 20,* or *100?* Go for it! See page 64 for a list of dictionaries and other resources.

the signs

## more

# more

## making the sign

*More* is a two-handed sign. Touch the fingers to the thumb on each hand. Then bring your hands together (fingers touching) twice in front of your chest.

## ready for more

*More* is one of the most popular signs and is the first of our **THREE GOLDEN SIGNS.** Try the activities below to put *more* in context.

- If baby finishes eating but still seems hungry, ask if she wants more while showing the sign. Then offer another bite.

- At playtime, try a similar technique with a bunch of blocks or balls. Take turns putting them into a big bowl. Before placing a toy in the bowl, ask, *More?* Repeat until all the toys are in the bowl.

- The playground is an excellent place to reinforce *more*. Place the child in a swing and give a gentle push. Then sign and ask, "Do you want more?" Then give another gentle push.

---

◆ **sign-o-nym**

**more kisses!** The signs for *kiss* and *more* look exactly the same except for one crucial difference: two taps for *more* and only one tap for *kiss*. Imagine each of your hands as a set of lips puckered up and ready to smooch. Then go for it!

---

# milk

# milk

## making the sign

*Milk* is a one-handed sign. Hold out your hand and open and close it twice as if you were squeezing something.

## thirsty for milk

*Milk*, the second of our **THREE GOLDEN SIGNS,** may well be your baby's first. It is easy to reinforce because it seems like an ever-present desire. At feeding time, show the sign before offering milk. Once your child learns this sign, expect to see it all the time! (If you are unable to reinforce the sign by giving your baby milk at that moment, you might want to quickly change the subject, or watch out for a flurry of fist squeezing.)

- If you see your baby making a fist, assume he's signing, encourage him and ask if he's saying *milk*.

> **■ asl tip**
>
> **whole milk** *Milk,* as shown here, is a relatively new sign. An older version is two handed and looks like you're milking a cow. The new sign is easier for kids to do and, we hope, does not give the impression that nursing moms are in any way similar to cattle.

# eat

# eat

## making the sign

With one hand, touch your fingers to your thumb (like *more*) and bring your hand, fingers first, to your mouth. It looks like you're eating with your hands.

## hungry?

*Eat* is the third and final sign of the **THREE GOLDEN SIGNS.** Any parent knows that most young children are constantly putting things in their mouths, so they've got good hand-to-mouth coordination already.

- Introduce the sign for *eat* during mealtime—not only for the obvious reasons but also because the high chair makes an excellent place to practice signing as you have a captive audience. Keep your eyes open for other places to sign where your baby is safe and content, such as the bathtub or the stroller.

> ■ **asl tip**
>
> **a question of expression** Now that you know the **THREE GOLDEN SIGNS,** how do you ask if your child wants something? To turn these signs into questions, raise your eyebrows in an inquiring way and make the sign. With question eyebrows, the sign for *eat* becomes: *Do you want to eat?* Facial expressions are very important in ASL.

# happy

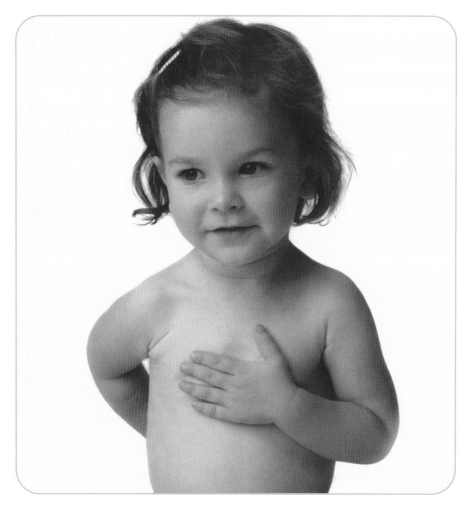

# happy

## making the sign

With an upward motion, touch your chest twice with your full hand, palm in. Don't forget to smile!

## is everybody happy?

This sign illustrates an important element of ASL: facial expression. (To sign *happy* with a frown is just plain sarcastic.) *Happy* is a great sign to introduce because babies are capable of the gesture, and it positively reinforces a joyful feeling. This and other feeling signs can help babies talk about their emotions.

■ **asl tip**

**tracks of my tears** Babies are very empathetic and often want to know why other babies are crying or screaming. This is a great opportunity to introduce the sign for *sad*: use your index fingers to trace the path of tears rolling down your cheeks.

● **music**

**sing and sign** Every parent knows firsthand how well babies respond to music, and that is why we use songs to teach babies (and parents) to sign. "The More We Get Together" is a favorite that incorporates two important signs, *more* and *happy*. "If You're Happy and You Know It" is another classic that is perfect for practicing *happy* and *sad*. You can use it to also introduce more signs by inventing new verses—check out one of the ASL dictionaries recommended on page 64.

mommy

# mommy

## making the sign

With your palm facing to the side, touch your chin twice with the thumb of your open hand.

## i want my mommy

*Mommy* is easy to learn, and it gets a lot of use. Babies love to identify the important people in their lives, and mommy is definitely *numbero uno*. (Sorry, dads—but don't worry, your time will come. Think of it as mommy's reward for surviving pregnancy.)

- A photo album is a great prop for practicing this and other family member signs. Point to people in the pictures as you sign. Pictures of families in other books work well too. Even walks in the park or trips to the store can be excellent mommy-, daddy-, and baby-spotting adventures.

---

**■ asl tip**

**baby sign** You probably already know the sign for *baby*. It's easy to do. Just turn your arms into a cradle and rock them back and forth.

---

**▲ look it up!**

**a family affair** All families are different. Make sure to show your child the signs for the family members present in your household. Check an ASL dictionary for the signs for *grandmother, grandfather, aunt, uncle, cousin, brother, sister,* or *babysitter*. See page 64 for a list of dictionaries and other resources.

# daddy

# daddy

## making the sign

With your palm facing to the side, touch the center of your forehead twice with the thumb of your open hand.

## father figure

Another easy sign, *daddy* looks just like *mommy* except the thumb taps the forehead instead of the chin. Try these games to reinforce *daddy*:

- Play a game of peek-a-boo with signs. Dad, hide your face and ask: "Where's Daddy?" Then uncover you face and make the sign, saying: *Here's Daddy!*

- Mirrors are great fun for babies: point to daddy in the mirror and make the sign.

- Point out mommies and daddies in picture books.

> ### ■ asl tip
>
> **not politically correct** In ASL the bottom half of the face is considered feminine and the top half of the face is masculine. So signs relating to girls and women are made below the nose while signs for boys and men are made above the nose. (ASL was developed before gender equality became the norm; we'll leave it to you to explain this to your kids!)

# book

# book

## making the sign

Put your palms together and then open them up as if they were the pages of a book. Imagine that the words are printed across your palms.

## little bookworms

This sign is great because it looks like what it is and it is very easy, so even the littlest signers can do it. Using storybooks to reinforce signs is lots of fun. For a very young baby, choose a colorful book with only one picture per page. Point to the image and sign as you say the word. Your child will be enchanted by the vividness of the experience. It's like adding moving images to the story.

- When reading ABC books, try using the ASL alphabet on page 4.

- Counting books are great practice. See page 5 for *1* to *10* in ASL.

Book-savvy toddlers love more-complicated illustrations and stories. Try substituting a sign for a recurring word in the story or use the point-and-sign method described above. You needn't sign all the words in a sentence to get a story idea across. Focus on the most obvious elements of a story or illustration and move into more detail as both your and your child's vocabulary increase.

# banana

# banana

## making the sign

Hold your index finger out in front of you and "peel" it using the thumb and forefinger of your other hand.

## yummy in my tummy

Food signs are a staple of Sign-a-Song. They are terrific starter signs because baby can see and recognize the object rather than having to understand a concept. This iconic sign looks just like what it is. Many children and adults naturally execute this sign without even knowing it, and children can acquire this sign early on because it's easy to make—and because bananas are a favorite snack.

### skip ahead
Everyone loves a polite child: see page 53 for "please."

## ▲ look it up!

**tasty vittles** Some foods, like *avocado* and *tofu,* have no specific sign. (In our opinion tofu has no specific flavor, either.) Others, like *cheese, berry, peas, grapes, carrots,* and *bread,* are easy to do. Have fun with food signs. Make sure you can sign your child's favorite foods. See page 64 for a list of dictionaries and other resources to help you learn new signs.

# apple

# apple

## making the sign

Twist the knuckle of your index finger into your cheek, like the dimple of an apple.

## an apple a day

We love food signs—and so do babies! Some kids are more interested in eating the foods than talking about them . . . and others have the opposite problem. Try giving baby a choice of fruits and making the sign to ask which one she wants.

> ❖ **game**
>
> **grocery grab** Gather five or six pieces of play food, pictures of food, or the real thing. Pretend you are at the store: select the foods, pay for them, bag them, take them home, and unpack them—using the signs all the while. Then see what happens next time baby recognizes the things at the supermarket.

> ■ **asl tip**
>
> **fruits and veggies** Many words in ASL are initialized. For *fruit,* make an *F*-hand. Bring it next to your mouth on the same side of your body and pivot the *F* back and forth where your thumb and index finger touch your face. For *vegetable,* use the same motion, but this time use the V-hand, with the tip of your index finger touching near your mouth.

# cracker

# cracker

## making the sign

Make a fist with one hand and position it in front of your opposite shoulder. Make an *A* with your other hand and use it to tap a few times near the elbow on the outside of your other arm.

## cracker snackers

Kids love crackers—all kinds of crackers. And this sign is generally a favorite because kids love the movement of it and it is surprisingly easy to remember.

---

❖ **game**

**shape sorter** Line up crackers of different shapes, and trace each shape in the air. See if your child can match your shape to the right cracker. For shapes with straight sides, start with your index fingers together at the center and top of the shape. Then trace the right and left sides of the shape simultaneously with your fingers ending up at the bottom center. For circles and ovals, outline the shape in the air with one index finger.

---

■ **asl tip**

**hey, cookie!** To sign *cookie,* hold one hand flat, palm up. The other acts as a cookie cutter, palm down, fingers curled. Pretend you are cutting cookies out of imaginary dough. Be prepared: baby may want more than an imaginary treat!

cat

# cat

## making the sign

Make whiskers by drawing an *F*-hand (see page 4) away from one side of your mouth.

## raining cats and dogs

Kids are naturally attracted to animals, especially their family pets. When you introduce the sign for *cat,* make sure to meow, too. By combining words, movements, and sounds, you can create a total sensory experience for your baby. After introducing signs for the local fauna, don't be surprised if your child wants to point out every animal in the neighborhood.

> ■ **asl tip**
>
> **good dog** To sign *dog,* pat your thigh with your open palm as if you were calling a dog. This is a modified sign. The real sign for *dog* ends with a finger snap. First, pat your thigh and then snap the fingers of the same hand. Since snapping is quite challenging for little ones, we omit it.

> ❖ **game**
>
> **zoo trip** Take a zoo trip or have a pretend zoo outing using stuffed animals. Ask, *What animals do you see?* Take turns signing and making animal noises to describe the animals you see. In a pretend zoo, cats and dogs can be found next to lions and tigers!

# bird

# bird

## making the sign
Open and close your thumb and index finger right in front of your mouth, just like a beak.

## early birds
*Bird* is a great early sign because it's the same as the pincer movement—a major milestone in fine motor skill development. This sign refers to all manner of small birds that you might see outside your window. Wrens, robins, starlings, cuckoos, and blue jays can be referred to using this blanket term. In ASL, birds are differentiated by following the *bird* sign with a characteristic, such as the robin's red breast or the blue feathers of a blue jay. For babies, however, the sign for *bird* is plenty.

### combine it!
bird + mommy = mommy bird
bird + daddy = daddy bird
bird + baby = baby bird

## ● music
**quacking chorus** "Six Little Ducks" is a great song to sing and quack. *Duck* looks like *bird* except the wide bill of the duck is portrayed by both the index and middle fingers as they open and close with the thumb. Use the *duck* sign every time you sing *duck* or *quack*.

# fish

# fish

## making the sign

Place the tip of one index finger on the palm of the other hand and wiggle the front fingers back and forth together as though your fingers were a fish wriggling through the water.

## the one that got away

Bath time is a great time to introduce many signs. Drop some plastic fish into the water and make the sign for *fish*. Try combining them with sizes—just indicate the size of the fish using your open hands, palms facing each other: *big fish, little fish*. If you want to use ASL grammar, follow the noun with adjectives: *fish big, fish little*.

### combine it!
### cracker + fish = fish cracker

---

### ▲ look it up!

**undersea signs** Oceans, lakes, and rivers are full of fun signs. *Dolphin, whale, octopus, shrimp,* and *crab* are some baby favorites. Arm yourself with these signs before a visit to the aquarium. See page 64 for a list of dictionaries and other resources.

# tiger

# tiger

## making the sign

Shape your fingers into claws. Start with the two hands, palms in, together in front of your face. Then move them across your face in opposite directions, tracing the tiger's stripes.

## wild child

Wild animal signs are really fun: they look like the animals they portray. This helps kids connect the sign to the animal. Remember to make the appropriate animal noises. *Tiger* can be accompanied by a ferocious growl or a gentle purr—depending on your child's disposition.

---

■ **asl tip**

**the elephant's trunk** Children love to sign *elephant*. Start with your hand at your nose, palm down, fingertips pointing forward. With a sloping curve down and away from your face, trace the shape of the elephant's trunk with your full hand. Elephants make a trumpeting sound that is sure to get a giggle!

---

■ **asl tip**

**z-o-o spells fun** *Zoo* is a spelled-out sign that many children can recognize and do. Spell *zoo* in the air by tracing a *Z* with your index finger. In one fluid motion, connect your fingers to make an *O* (see page 4) and move it a few inches to the right. All double letters are indicated in this way, though most don't follow the letter *Z*.

# flower

# flower

## making the sign

Make an *O* with one hand (see page 4). Use that hand to touch your fingertips to your upper lip twice, once underneath each nostril, as though you were smelling a flower.

## everything's coming up noses

*Flower* can refer to any flower. Some flowers, such as roses (see asl tip), have a specific sign. Like the sign for *bird*, the general sign *flower* will suffice for most babies. Take your child on a real or imaginary garden tour and "sniff" all the flowers in this way.

- It's great to get into a routine of practicing signing with your baby at the same time (when he is happiest) or during the same activity (when she is most relaxed). For some babies, that time is when you are out for a stroll. If you and your baby get into the habit of signing while on walks, your sign vocabulary will increase quickly.

> **■ asl tip**
>
> **flower power** Here's a great example of an initialized sign. *Rose* is made by substituting an *R*-hand for the *O*-hand while making the sign for *flower*.

# tree

# tree

## making the sign

Place the elbow of one arm on the palm of your other hand. With your palm facing the side, spread your fingers as though they were the branches of the tree and shake it out a bit. There's a nice breeze coming through.

## one, two, tree

Whether you're a city or a country family, chances are there are at least a few trees around for you to point to during signing practice. But if not, picture books will help.

- Now that you know that the *tree* motion is more than just a snazzy dance move, ask your child, *Who lives in a tree? A bird?* (Yes!) *Who lives in a tree? A tiger?* (No!) Have fun using animal noises and being silly.

> ### ■ asl tip
>
> **tree's a crowd** Is your child more interested in the forest than the tree? No problem. Just move the sign for *tree* from left to right. Don't forget to shake the leaves (your fingers). Want to make the sign for *jungle*? Just let your branches go limp—make them sway, and you have the sagging treetops of the jungle.

# train

# train

## making the sign

Hold out a *U*-hand, palm down. With your other hand, make another *U* and place it across the other. Rub the top fingers up and down the length of the bottom ones. Your bottom hand represents the two iron rails, and the top hand looks like the railroad ties going by.

## all aboard

Some kids like trains, and others are obsessed with them. Either way, this general sign can be used for subways, passenger trains, freight trains, and toy trains. Yes, even blue tank engines are covered by this humble sign.

---

■ **asl tip**

**a body in motion** In ASL, if you want to show that the train is going somewhere you need to use a classifier. For trains, cars, buses, or trucks, use a 3-hand to represent the vehicle. Move your hand, fingers first, in the direction the vehicle is moving. Say, "There goes the train! Woo-woo!"

---

❖ **game**

**counting all cars** Toy trains are not necessary for this game—even a drawing will work. Make a train and count the cars. Start with a short train and work your way up to ten cars. Point to each car as you say and sign the number.

# airplane

# airplane

## making the sign

With your palm facing down, bend only the middle and ring fingers toward your palm. Then fly your hand around the room.

## ready for take-off

Playing airplane is fun. Use your signing hand to take off, land, and fly all over the place. Be sure to supply the roar of the engines! Expand your story. Fly over trees and flowers. Look down and see the cats and tigers below. Serve an onboard meal (four dollars; exact change is appreciated) of apples and crackers. To land, fly the plane down onto your upturned palm. Take off from the same position.

### ■ asl tip

**sky high** *Helicopter* is another sign that will fly with most kids. Place one hand, palm down, on top of your other hand's index finger, which is pointing up. Wobble your top hand to show the motion of the rotors, and don't forget the noises!

### ■ asl tip

**blast off!** Imagine leaving Earth in a rocket ship. Hold up one hand, fingers up and palm facing the side. This is part of the launch pad. With your other hand, make an *R*, with your fingertips pointing upward—the rocket. Place the rocket up against the launch pad. Count down and then blast off by raising your *R*-hand into the air.

# boat

# boat

## making the sign

Cup your hands together in the shape of a boat. Don't forget to bob the boat up and down; there's choppy water ahead.

## ship shape

A lot of parents ask, isn't *boat* the same as *book*? They do look similar, but there are two significant differences: the shape of the hands (*boat* hands are cupped a bit) and motion (*boat* hands move forward). But the key difference is context: "Michael, Row Your Book Ashore" just doesn't make sense!

❖ **game**

**bon voyage** Plan a signed adventure. Tell your child that you're going to take a pretend journey, somewhere far, far away. First, get on a boat. After the boat comes ashore, switch to a train, then a plane, and finally a rocket. Sound effects are essential. Exercise your lips and make those motor sounds.

● **music**

**sculling song** "Row, Row, Row Your Boat" is a great song to sign. Just add the boat and rowing action and you're in business. Hint: *merry* is the same sign as *happy*.

hat

# hat

## making the sign

Tap the top of your head twice with the palm of one hand.

## hats off!

*Hat* is a frequent first sign. It's easy to do, and hats are an ever-present feature of a baby's life. What you may not have realized is that if something is on your head—no matter how outrageous—it must be a hat. Place a banana on top of your head and say, "Look at me: I have a banana hat!" Then do the signs. Repeat with other objects. The more outrageous the better—silliness is definitely a plus.

> ## ▲ look it up!
>
> **clothes minded** If your child is interested in fashion, try teaching the signs for *shirt, skirt, dress, pants,* and *clothing.* Then hit the boutiques. See page 64 for a list of dictionaries and other resources.

> ## ■ asl tip
>
> **polite to point** The signs for external body parts are as easy as a well-directed point. Just point at your toe to sign *toe.* Point at your eye to sign *eye.* Remember that it is considered more polite to point at the body part in question on your own body rather than someone else's.

# shoes

# shoes

## making the sign

Make two fists, palms down, and tap them together twice in front of your body.

## shoe business

This is another fabulously graphic sign. It looks like two shoes sitting happily together on the closet floor. Teach this sign by exaggerating the movement of the two shoes coming together. Include a sound effect like *ka-pow*. It's enough like clapping that most kids can perform this sign easily. Use it to lighten the mood at the shoe store or any time the putting-on of shoes meets with resistance!

> ❖ **game**
>
> **whose shoes?** This is a great way to combine signs and to get lots of giggles. Children love to try on other people's shoes. The bigger the better. Place Mommy's or Daddy's shoes on your baby's feet and ask, *Whose shoes?* Sign *mommy shoes.* Try an assortment of shoes, big and small, followed by the appropriate signed combination. Finally, offer your child the opportunity to clunk around in his or her new, magnificent footwear.

love

# love

## making the sign

Make *A*-hands and cross both arms across your chest.
Let the love show in your face, too!

## i love you

It's never too early to introduce the word *love* into your child's vocabulary! This is a wonderful sign to practice and is best done with smiles and cuddles. When it is time to drop off your little one at a playgroup or school, signing *I love you* often makes for a smoother exit—not to mention it is just plain easier to sign across a crowded and noisy playground.

- There are many ways to say *I love you* in sign language (or in any language for that matter): Why not try them all? For little kids, the easiest is probably to point to yourself for *I*, add *love*, and then point to the lucky receiver for *you*. You can blow a kiss or use your middle fingers to trace a heart on your chest (which also means *valentine*) to show even those who don't know sign language how much they mean to you.

---

◆ **sign-o-nym**

**i love airplanes!** Want to see some magic? Turn an airplane into an *I love you*. Just make an airplane (see page 41) and flip your wrist so that your palm faces out—you'll be signing *I love you*. This amazing sign incorporates the first three letters of *I love you*, *I*, *L*, and *Y*, simultaneously. That's the short way to say it. One sign, one love!

---

# nice

# nice

## making the sign

Hold one hand in front of you, palm facing up. Put your palms together and slide your top hand to the tips of your bottom fingers.

## nice try

Okay, this sign is more for parents than for kids. Use *nice* as a reminder or encouragement when disciplining. You may find that using this discreet sign as a silent advance warning can actually defuse a potential tantrum—saving both you and your little one lots of embarrassment. The tricky part is getting your child to look at you before you sign.

To teach this sign, try gently moving your baby's hands into position, so she understands how the soft touch of the palm rub exemplifies the feeling of *nice*. Move her hands and repeat the word until you sense that she gets the idea.

◆ **sign-o-nym**

**nice and clean** The sign for *nice* is also used for *neat* and *clean*. To say *tidy*, the sign looks the same except you repeat the motion. See page 55 for more about bath time.

# please

# please

## making the sign

Put your palm over your heart and move your whole hand in a big circle on your chest.

## if you please

Teaching a child to say *please* is one of the big challenges of parenting. It is also very rewarding—a polite child is a great pleasure to be around! The best teacher, of course, is imitation: if you always say and sign *please* (and *thank you*, see below for how), your baby will want do it, too. But if it becomes an issue, and you find that your child is unwilling to use the word *please* on principle, he may be willing to use the sign as a compromise. You'll have to keep your eyes on him or you'll miss it!

> ### ■ asl tip
> **magic words** To sign *thank you*, simply touch your chin with the tips of your fingers, then extend your hand forward—almost as if blowing a kiss. To sign *sorry*, curl your fingers into an A-hand (see page 4), then move your hand in a circle on your chest. For both signs the appropriate facial expression is a must.

> ### ◆ sign-o-nym
> **good stuff** *Yummy* is a universal sign. Move your open hand in a circular motion around your tummy—just like *please*, but tastier.

# bath

# bath

## making the sign

Make two *A*-hands and simultaneously rub them up and
down both sides of your chest, as if you were scrubbing.

## clean-up time

*Bath* is a popular sign for kids who really love their baths. Bath time is a regular occur-
rence, so you should have lots of opportunities to practice the sign. The tub is a great
place to practice other signs as well. While baby sits and plays, you could talk about boats,
birds, or fish. Body parts are also in plain view for signing practice.

---

**■ asl tip**

**lather up!** *Shampoo* is fun and easy to learn because it's one of those signs that
looks just like the action: put your hands up to your head as if lathering your hair.

---

**■ asl tip**

**when you gotta go** The sign for *potty* or *toilet* is shaking a *T*-hand from left to
right. This is a great sign for those of you who are introducing potty training to
your youngsters and particularly helpful if your child is a bit shy when
approached in pubic about the subject. Raise your eyebrows to turn it into a
question: *Do you have to go potty?*

# bed

# bed

## making the sign

Place palms and fingers together and rest your cheek on the outside of a hand.

## sleepytime

*Bed* is not the most popular sign with babies but is much requested and needed by parents. To put *bed* in context, talk to your child about what you do together at night. Perhaps your evening begins with dinner. Okay, that's *eating time*. The sign for *time* is made by pointing with your index finger at the back of your wrist, right where you'd expect to see a watch. What happens after eating time? Bath time? Book time? Bed time? Nighty-night!

---

### ■ asl tip

**sleep vs. tired** The sign for *sleep* refers to the action of sleeping (verb) or the condition of being drowsy or sleepy (adjective), like you might feel after a satisfying meal. To sign *sleep,* place your open hand in front of your face, fingers apart and palm in. Then draw your hand straight down to chest level, closing your fingers until they touch your thumb. *Tired* refers to the way you feel at the end of the day—you know, just plain exhausted—or, in the context of a baby's day, ready for a long nap. To sign *tired,* put your fingers just below your shoulders, elbows sticking out a bit, and shrug down. Imagine a bird folding its wings to go to sleep.

---

# night

# night

## making the sign

Hold one arm out level in front of you, palm facing down. This is the horizon. To show the setting sun, curve the fingers of your other hand and lower your forearm so that the fingers pass in front of your outstretched arm.

## owl through the night

*Night* is a terrific sign because it presents in miniature the setting of the sun. Children seem to understand this sign intuitively and reproduce it easily.

- A good way to reinforce this sign is to talk about what else happens at night. Can baby see the moon from her window? The sign for moon is a *C*-hand (like a crescent moon) tapping the side of the forehead and moving upward toward the sky.

- Owls are up at night (like babies). To sign *owl,* place *O*-hands in front of your eyes and peer through. Whoooooo's awake tonight? It's owl! And you!

■ **asl tip**

**first light** The sun rising and setting is beautiful to watch, and so are the signed versions. To sign *morning,* stretch one arm (the sun) out straight in front of you, palm up. Place your other palm, facing down, in the crook of your elbow. Raise the sun arm so that the palm comes up to face you. Be careful with this sign; it looks like something else!

stop

# stop

## making the sign

Hold one hand in front of you, palm up, fingers pointing to the side. Bring the side of the other hand sharply down against it, fingers together and pointing forward. It looks like a karate chop. This parent-of-toddlers-requested sign is also adored by children.

## stop! who goes there?

To practice *stop,* it's good to know how to sign *go,* too. Use both index fingers to point in the direction you intend to go. Play stop-and-go games to reinforce these signs.

- With your baby in a swing, stroller, or carrier, play stop-and-go together. Sign and say *go* and begin walking, dancing, jumping—whatever. Sign and say *Stop* and stop the activity. You may well induce some giggles.

- With a toddler or a group of toddlers, pick an activity—like jumping, marching, or spinning—and sign and say *Go.* Stop them with the spoken word and sign for *stop.* Repeat with different motions until your children beg for mercy.

Sign these activities with verbal cues first and then sign silently to strengthen your child's observation skills.

> ■ asl tip
>
> **a good start** The signs contained in this book are just a beginning. To get the most out of this beautiful language, participate in a course in which you and your child can practice and build on the signs shown here with other signers.

# afterword: signing, talking, communicating

Any one of the signs shown in this book could be your child's first or favorite. *Milk, more,* and *eat*—our three golden signs—are unfailingly popular. The child who loves bath time will squeal with delight when he sees *bath*. For your youngster a hat may bring on a flurry of head patting and giggling. Keep an eye on what appeals to your baby and use those signs the most. Once your child gets the idea, her capacity to recognize and duplicate signs may increase very rapidly.

Once your child begins to speak, there will be no stopping him. The flood of words may quickly drown out all of the signs you learned together. Problem? Not at all. Baby signing is just the beginning, a way to encourage baby's natural urge to communicate and expose him to a language you both can use. If you want to continue signing with your child, the most important thing is to keep signing yourself. These ideas may help:

- Try signing silently. Play a game in which no one is allowed to speak out loud.

- Encourage your child to teach her signs to someone else. A younger sibling or friend makes a great pupil.

- Add to your sign vocabulary. Find fun ways to introduce new signs to your child that reflect his interests. Soon you may be asked for new signs.

- Use the ASL alphabet to help your child learn to recognize printed letters. Junior may still recognize a signed *A* faster than a written one. Try a similar approach to learning to read numbers and basic addition.

- Use signs like *eat* and *potty* to communicate in an environment where yelling across a room or playground could be embarrassing.

- Keep it fun!

# resources

Take your child's signing to the next level with these fantastic resources. Don't forget: your child will only be as enthusiastic about signing as you are!

## picture books with signs

These sign language picture books use American Sign Language, which we encourage.

*The Handmade Alphabet* by Laura Rankin
A beautifully illustrated sign language alphabet book.

*Moses Goes to a Concert, Moses Goes to School,* and *Moses Goes to the Circus* by Isaac Millman
Wonderful stories about a child who is deaf. Written in English and American Sign Language with illustrations and detailed diagrams of signs.

## picture books without signs

The colorful pictures and simple language of these books lead to many engaging signing activities.

*Brown Bear, Brown Bear, What Do You See?* by Bill Martin Jr. and Eric Carle

*Doggies* by Sandra Boyton

*Hug* by Jez Alborough

*Fish Eyes: A Book You Can Count On* by Lois Ehlert

*Good Night, Gorilla* by Peggy Rathmann

*The Very Busy Spider* by Eric Carle

## sign language dictionaries

*Random House Webster's American Sign Language Dictionary* by Elaine Costello

*Signs for Me: Basic Sign Vocabulary for Children, Parents, and Teachers* by Ben Bahan and Joe Dannis

## sign language for children

*Dancing with Words: Signing for Hearing Children's Literacy* by Marilyn Daniels
Great text for educators and parents of emerging readers or children who have reading disabilities.

## familiar songs to sing with your children

These are wonderful songs to sing with your children. It is not necessary to sign every word, only the words that have the most meaning to your child.

"If You're Happy and You Know It": With each new verse, change *happy* to another feeling sign.

"I Love My Rooster": With each new verse, change the animal sign.

"The More We Get Together": A great song for practicing *more* and *happy*.

"The Wheels on the Bus": You can substitute *bus* for any other vehicle that your child is focused on.

## web sites

www.masterstech-home.com/ASLDict.html, *A Basic Dictionary of ASL Terms*: This Web site has QuickTime videos of people signing; it's great for seeing the signs that involve movement!

www.sign-a-song.com, *Sign-a-Song: A Musical Introduction to American Sign Language for Babies and Their Caregivers*: Our Web site has information regarding Sign-a-Song workshops and events.

## music for signing

See www.sign-a-song.com for more details.

*More!:* Ten original and traditional songs from our popular Sign-a-Song workshops.

*My Bed Is an Airplane:* More original songs from our popular Sign-a-Song workshops.

# meet the authors

**Andrea Fixell** has a master's degree from Teachers College, Columbia University, in deaf education. Since 1991 she has been a teacher of deaf and hard-of-hearing students and an educator for deaf adults. In 2001, Andrea, then a new mother, started a sign language class for parents and babies. Because of its popularity, she was soon joined by **Ted Stafford,** guitarist and parent. Ted, who has a background in educational publishing, teaches guitar and music theory as well as performs for children and adults. Together, Andrea and Ted, whose zany chemistry and original songs are a hallmark of their Sign-a-Song workshops, have taught sign language to thousands of babies and toddlers.

## acknowledgments

Thank you very much to all of the children, parents, and caregivers who participated in the photo shoots. Special thanks to Phoebe Braun, Maddy Penalver, Luca Rodas, Lucas Simpson, Veronique Kinser, and Alexander Crowther, who were photographed but do not appear in this book.

Thanks also to the many families who have included us and Sign-a-Song in this special time in their children's lives. We are so fortunate to have your support and love.

# meet the signers

abby

alex

ari

azana

coco

dashiell

elias

ella

ella

jai

jessica

kate

kim

lea

lila

lola

mabel

maeve

mondriana

nathaniel

noa

noah

olivia

raina

sam

siobahn

sofia

washington

waverly

zeb

# index

Page numbers in *italics* indicate fully illustrated signs